BETWEEN SPACES

WE ALSO SEE SPECTATORS WATCHING (THEM) IN INTERCUT SEQUENCES. THEY ARE, IT WOULD SEEM, LOOKING AT WHAT WE SEE. THERE IS, AT LEAST, AS IN ALL MONTAGE SEQUENCES OF THIS SORT, THE IMPLICATION OF A SPECTACLE SHARED BY FILMED SPECTATOR AND SPECTATOR OF THE FILM.... THE IMPLICATION OF SHARED SPECTACLE IS THEREFORE SUBVERTED, AND ONE IS MADE CONSCIOUS OF THIS DISJUNCTION.

—ANNETTE MICHELSON, "THE MAN WITH THE MOVIE CAMERA, FROM MAGICIAN TO EPISTEMOLOGIST," *ARTFORUM* MARCH 1972

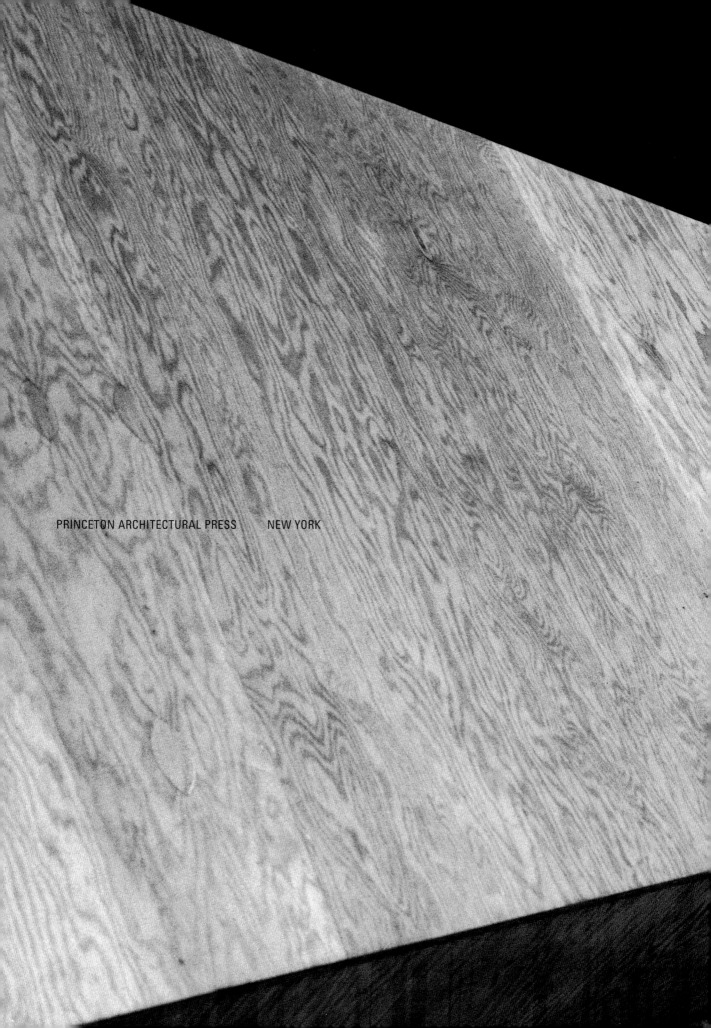

PRINCETON ARCHITECTURAL PRESS   NEW YORK

BETWEEN SPACES

SMITH-MILLER+HAWKINSON ARCHITECTURE
JUDITH TURNER PHOTOGRAPHY

PUBLISHED BY
PRINCETON ARCHITECTURAL PRESS
37 EAST 7TH STREET
NEW YORK, NEW YORK 10003
212 995 9620

LIBRARY OF CONGRESS
CATALOGING-IN-PUBLICATION DATA
BETWEEN SPACES: SMITH-MILLER + HAWKINSON
ARCHITECTURE, JUDITH TURNER PHOTOGRAPHY
P.CM.
ISBN 1-56898-227-5 (ALK. PAPER)
1. SMITH-MILLER + HAWKINSON ARCHITECTS. 2.
ARCHITECTURE-UNITED STATES. 3. ARCHITECTURE,
MODERN-20TH CENTURY-UNITED STATES. 4.
ARCHITECTURAL PHOTOGRAPHY-UNITED STATES.
I. TURNER, JUDITH. II. SMITH-MILLER + HAWKINSON
ARCHITECTS.
NA737.S579 B48 2000
720'.92'2-DC21
                                    99-053586
                                         CIP

PROJECT EDITOR: BETH HARRISON
DESIGN: DIETER JANSSEN
RESEARCH: AMANDA REESER

FOR A FREE CATALOGUE OF BOOKS,
CALL 800 722 6657
VISIT OUR WEBSITE AT WWW.PAPRESS.COM

SPECIAL THANKS TO: ANN ALTER, EUGENIA BELL,
JAN CIGLIANO, JANE GARVIE, CAROLINE GREEN,
CLARE JACOBSON, LESLIE ANN KENT, MARK LAMSTER,
ANNE NITSCHKE, LOTTCHEN SHIVERS, SARA E.
STEMEN, JENNIFER THOMPSON, AND DEB WOOD OF
PRINCETON ARCHITECTURAL PRESS

                        KEVIN LIPPERT, PUBLISHER

CONTENTS

TEXTS

PROJECTION IS NOT A THING IN ITSELF BUT A RELATIONSHIP BETWEEN THINGS.... PROJECTION OPERATES IN THE INTERVALS BETWEEN THINGS. IT IS ALWAYS TRANSITIVE.

—ROBIN EVANS, *THE PROJECTIVE CAST*, 1995

HENRY SMITH-MILLER + LAURIE HAWKINSON

BETWEEN SPACES

It is possible that an architectural detail can reveal more than just the resolution of materials. A fragment of a building can provide an entrance into a particular way of thinking. A detail can be seen as a kind of evidence, a piece of evidentiary material; building can therefore be the result of the building up of this material evidence.

The six built projects represented in this book are both autonomous and over-lapping investigations into the development and meaning of materials, as well as into the relationship of an architectural program to the materials and surfaces that are used to create space. These investigations persist through shifts in project scale. From the several-hundred-square-foot installation for the *Fabrications* exhibit at the Museum of Modern Art in New York to the renovation of a Manhattan loft for Bob Greenberg and Corvova Lee, from the successive additions to a house in California to the Corning Glass Center in Corning, from the ferry terminal at Wall Street to the two-acre Amphitheatre and Outdoor Cinema at the North Carolina Museum of Art—each project is invested in the conventional historical conjunction of materials, program, and site.

Corning Glass Center 2000, a project completed in June 1999, simultaneously represents the research work of Corning and our own research into the meaning of glass as an architectural material. The entry facade is comprised of a curtain wall that utilizes a mullion-less, point-fitting system together with a series of very thin and light stainless steel vertical trusses. At times these trusses are placed outside the building envelope and at other times they are inside, producing an oscillating zone that essentially thickens "perimeter" as an idea. Contrary to typical curtain wall con-struction, the visitor does not enter the building at right angles to the facade, but rather slips between the walls. The thin green edge of the glass is the first surface the visitor sees and the experience of entry is thus attenuated and didactic. Glass and its

history become both the structure and the content of the museum.

Also at Corning, we designed a theater with a glass screen so that glass, again, performs doubly as transparent surface (window) and a surface for reflection (screen). The circumstance is local, but our concern is the larger historical frame within in which glass has a variety of meanings—from an *invisible* material that provides enclosure and security, to a modernist material that signifies lightness and gravity simultaneously, to a *unit* in the economic building systems of later modernism.

As an addition to an addition, *Outside In* magnifies a density of relationships. The project acknowledges and identifies by design, a continuously evolving domestic condition. The original house and its configuration physically and formally inform subsequent additions. The appropriation of a prior condition brings, in part, prior context. By necessity—as in the cases of footings and foundations, or covenant and zoning setback laws—these conditions carry with them the cultural and social mores under which they were created. At the same time the addition responds to current needs, which in turn reflect current social organizations. The final project, while appearing casually assembled, is actually a carefully crafted weave of the new and a re-presented old.

Lastly, the cultural context of the Museum of Modern Art in New York permits an uncontaminated realization of our architectural research. By establishing the site as the viewer's eye and coordinating material effects with the construction of a projected space, we explored the correlation between the cultural institution and its architecture.

Collaboration operates not only among architects, but also cuts across hierarchies and disciplines in our work with artists, landscape architects, structural engineers, and even institutions. Our collaboration with Judith Turner, in this publication, defines a project that performs an additional operation on our work. Judith Turner's photographs are not straightforward pictures of architecture. The process of photographing for Judith Turner is similar and sympathetic to the architect's process of design. Framing, light and lightness, the relationship of planes in space, the juxtaposition of forms and materials are some of the similarities in our processes. Her photographs are of fragments, and architects design in fragments. The photographs recombine the found material and operate as a re-presentation of the architecture. The photographer materializes light and shadow as elements equal in weight to that of planes and solids in the architectural composition.

Judith Turner's photographs re-frame and therefore reveal to us once more our investment in a space that is projected from the alignments and lineaments of light and material.

JUDITH TURNER

OUT OF CONTEXT

I am not an architectural photographer. I am a photographer who uses architecture as subject matter to explore many of the formal concepts of the creative process. As I photograph buildings I attempt to reveal the poetry, essence, and structure of architecture.

My work is always composed of studies of multiple images of buildings, rather than a few recordings of their overall exterior and interior views. It is not possible to see or to comprehend architecture in its full complexity all at once. Architecture is an unfolding experience: a series of images can best convey some of the ideas and intentions inherent in a building.

There is a strong emphasis on and celebration of ambiguity in my photographs. My images often depict foreground as background, and vice versa. A solid becomes a void, causing the positive and negative to be transposed. Curved forms appear to flatten out. Scale is intentionally distorted and perspective is exaggerated. Gravity, itself, is defied in many of the photographs.

I photograph fragments—isolated parts, detached pieces, small sections— of buildings. When a fragment is recorded, it is taken out of context and loses its relationship to what it was. Inevitably it becomes something else, assuming a new meaning. The subject is decomposed and recreated through this reinterpretation. I am, therefore, always working on two levels. On one level, I endeavor to be true to the architecture and the intent behind it. On the other hand, I am creating my own divergent dream worlds of architecture.

A GLASS ARCHITECTURE EXHIBITION WOULD
HAVE TO BE LINKED TO THE EXPERIMENTAL
SITE, AND IT WOULD HAVE TO BE PERMANENT.
—PAUL SCHEERBART, *GLASS ARCHITECTURE*, 1914

JOHN HEJDUK

MEMORIES:THOUGHTS:IMAGES

1 One late afternoon this fall I was sitting with a good friend in the Book Store Room of the Canadian Centre for Architecture. We were talking about architecture and life. Within the calm room the only other inhabitant was the librarian. My friend and I were looking out a beautifully proportioned window that overlooked the entry courtyard. In our view, some thirty feet away, was a Canadian maple tree. The colors of the leaves were bright red and orange, some yellow. The daylight filtered through the glass of the window and made the room give off an atmosphere of subtle silence. The books held their secrets. On leaving this mysterious ambience, I obtained a new book entitled *Le Corbusier: Photographs by René Burri: Moments in the Life of a Great Architect*, edited and with a text by Arthur Rüegg.

2 On the journey (with another good friend) back to the airport, the driver of the car gave us a very special gift. He drove us along the old Montréal canal. This ride had great impact on me and my companion. The canal had on both sides of its banks a straight row of old poplar trees. As we moved past them, it was like seeing a filmstrip. The enclosing trees acted as still, cinemagraphic frames. The most extraordinary thing was that one felt one was in France, a compelling moment of light, movement, and landscape. The linear trip along the canal provoked memories, thoughts, images. The French Canadian driver asked us if we knew who brought the poplars to the North American continent. We said we did not know. He smiled and said, "Thomas Jefferson."

3 When I returned home, I immediately opened the book of photographs taken of Le Corbusier, and the persons and places upon which he built his architectures, his life. This book of photos is a very profound book. Of course I have seen photos of Le Corbusier, but this book completely changed my image of him. The photos revealed the man in the most unexpected way. Someone I never met and did not know became another reality, someone deliciously different. The photographer, Burri, caught something wonderful. The series with Heidi Weber is absolutely joyous, showing the depth of the human smile. Who can ever forget Le Corbusier tipping his hat at the Dominican Brothers at La Tourette? Or going over the monastery's working drawings, pencil in hand, hat on head, walking through the building site with a piece of straw in hand. And of course, Burri's magnificent bird's-eye view of the overwhelming power of the Chapel funnels....You can hear the Handel trumpets. Glory to God! and to the architect! and to Ronchamp, one of the great mysteries of life!...Children climbing up an inclined plane at the Cité Radieuse. Marseilles. And finally, the photo of Le Corbusier, standing straight and tall in the frame of two partitions in his apartment at 24 rue Nungesser et Coli, dressed in dark suit and vest, white shirt, dark bow tie, and on his lips a becoming, tentative smile. Books are also made to adjust one's thinking. In this case, it particularly changed my view about photography and architecture.

4 In 1975, when I was completing the Cooper Union Foundation Building renovation, my friend the painter and teaching colleague Robert Slutzky suggested that I meet with Judith Turner, a photographer. I did so, and was completely taken by this artist's photos. The Cooper Union commissioned Judith to do a photographic essay on the completed Foundation Building. Judith's photos captured the spirit of place and she produced beautiful, subtle, haunting photographs. That was twenty-five years ago. Since that time, she has become one of the preeminent architectural photographers in the world. Some years after photographing the Cooper Union she produced her own book, *Judith Turner Photographs Five Architects*, for which I was asked to write the introduction. The essay was entitled "The Flatness of Depth." Judith became a good friend.

A few months ago Laurie Hawkinson, partner of the studio of Smith-Miller + Hawkinson Architects, asked me if I would write an introduction to a book of Smith-Miller + Hawkinson work photographed by Judith Turner. Of course I said I would, for I had great admiration for Smith-Miller + Hawkinson's architectural work and Judith Turner's photographic work.

In preparation for doing this present essay, I reread the one I did for Judith's book twenty years ago, and decided to incorporate Part III (with some adjustments) regarding Judith's photography. Part III still holds and I still feel the same way about Judith's artistry.

"PART III

At first appearances, the subject of Judith Turner's photographs is architecture, although the meaning of the photographs (outside of their visual beauty and superb compositional precision) has to do with the degree of abstraction. To what extent does the subject matter (architecture) hold to its own inner essence? What kind of dialogue is going on between the observer (Judith Turner) and the observed (architecture)? Is it possible to capture the very essence of a subject in a single still photograph? Perhaps an additional inquiry could be, Why does Judith Turner focus on the fragments (details) of architecture? This leads us to the overwhelming question: When the subject matter is in fact abstract to begin with, does it survive further abstraction, or does a profound transformation take place?

Turner understands that it is impossible to see architecture in its full complexity at once. Architecture is made of details, fragments, fabrications. And the very idea behind it can be captured in a fragment, in a detail. And architecture is made up of two dimensions, and Mondrian understood this profoundly. Judith Turner does believe that the very essence of the spirit of an architecture can be captured in a single still photograph. She also knows that there is a precarious balance between the representation of the subject and its realities. In some cases, the further abstraction is pushed;

it de-materializes the very subject of its existence. The most profound architectures carry the same seed, the same essences, whatever realities they are "re-presented" in.

Judith Turner is able to re-present the abstraction and the substantive materiality of the subject matter in a dialectic of her own vision of realities, her own vision of photography as a creative act. Hers is the creation of a single still photograph of haunting visual beauty.

Judith Turner is also making a critical commentary on that which she photographs. Her art has to do with fixed silences upon abstracted thoughts. She searches for an unforgettable moment, like it or not, and she reveals sparsities and densities—the basic substance of architecture.

She is in love with white, black, and gray, and the way light washes surface in gentle ways. She informs opaque surfaces and translucent ones too. She is fascinated by the juxtaposition of the forms and shapes of architecture, the vocabulary of the elements of the elemental. She is obsessed by stairs, handrails, skylights, windows, columns, and beams, the way things fit together, the way they argue. She wants her solitary viewer to know that architecture is abstract, is still life. The materiality of glass, cement, plaster, steel, aluminium, wood, and galvanized metal is celebrated and honored through her photography; her silent witness is the photograph.

Judith Turner's vision is subtle, precise, impeccable, exacting, abstract, compositional, and quietly moving. She senses the materiality and the details. She knows space, and she is able to re-present it into something of her own, into another creative reality. Her photographs provoke thought in depth. She captures still moments. Judith Turner is an artist of rare creative sensibilities, and we are the recipients of her gifts."

Judith gives tender, loving care to the depths of Smith-Miller + Hawkinson architecture.

5 The first time I met Laurie Hawkinson was when we installed an exhibition of my Texas House drawings at the Institute for Architecture and Urban Studies. Laurie was Head of Exhibitions at the Institute. What struck me then was her energy, her precision, her craftmanship, her intelligence, and her determination, and she was wonderful to work with. The last thing I remember was Laurie lifting large panels of glass (and they were large) and gently placing them over the structure containing the drawings. It seems like yesterday; the year was 1980. Laurie entered the Cooper Union School of Architecture, and in the thesis class, she created one of the most memorable and profound works, called Cinetrain, in 1983. Her thesis was shown in the book *Education of an Architect*, Volume II, which the Irwin S. Chanin School of Architecture of the Cooper Union published in 1988. Laurie's statement of the program of Cinetrain follows:

The cinematic apparatus is comprised of eight parts for the production and projection of film. The Cinetrain conforms to the traveling dimensions of the railroad; cars are ten feet wide and all parts fold to be less than fourteen feet in height. The cars are chosen from existing railroad car types: the projector car, camera car, and chair car are derived from the work car; the seating car from the long flatbed car; and the screen car from the standard flatbed car.

The tracks of the railroad are the site. The Cinetrain carries film to a chosen site and unfolds for use. The participants board the train to view the film. The Cinetrain is also a machine for making film, and an educational tool for learning about the filmmaking process. The eight parts combine in a variety of ways for filming, editing, and viewing. The Cinetrain may operate perpendicular to the track so that the cars operate in a "field." In this configuration the cinematic apparatus simultaneously films, edits, and projects, resulting in a process through which spectator becomes both actor and audience.

THE CAMERA CAR

The subject. The camera can rotate and fix itself 360 degrees in any direction. The camera chair moves forward and back on the gantry arm. The film room under the gantry is for the temporary storage of films.

SCREEN CAR

The object. The screen car has four positions. The screen is able to rotate 360 degrees but may be fixed only at 90-degree positions, either parallel or perpendicular to the track.

PROJECTOR CAR

The projector car can project up to three films/images simultaneously. This car is able to rotate 360 degrees from zero to ten feet in elevation.

TRAM CAR

The tram transports viewers/participants to the seating car, and then from the seating car to any other car.

EDITING CAR

The editing car contains five rooms for editing film. Work being done in the editing car is visible through the screen from the outside. Screen, chair, and editing table are movable on the track running the width of the car.

CHAIR CAR

The object. The chair moves radically 360 degrees but can be fixed at 45-degree positions only. The chair can also slide forward and backward on the radial tracks.

SEATING CAR

The subject. Seating rotates 360 degrees, but as the screen, may only be fixed at positions perpendicular or parallel to the track. Access to the seating car is possible from stairs or from the tram car.

EQUIPMENT CAR

A standard boxcar for bringing lights, props, film, or any other film apparatus to the film/cinema site.

6 In reviewing Smith-Miller + Hawkinson's North Carolina Museum of Art Amphitheater and Outdoor Cinema, I was very interested in the four-legged film projection cube booth. This work is like some strange animal who comes out of a savannah and looks across at an outdoor screen. The night animal projects light into the night, onto the screens—its own night thoughts—and when it has done with its fleeting images shuts its own light off and stands there, sleeping silently until the next night.

7 I was invited to lecture at the University of Virginia in 1981. I met Henry Smith-Miller in Charlottesville, where he was a visiting professor. Henry Smith-Miller and I had supper together and talked about the place and architecture. The next day, I went to see Jefferson's Monticello. When I arrived at the top of the site, it appeared that Jefferson might have sliced the top of the mountain off…perhaps not. What I was not prepared for was the power of the house itself, a remarkable phenomenon. For the first time I understood the word "organic"…this ingenious work was still digesting…still alive! And it overlooked a magnificent Arcadian landscape right out of a Poussin painting.

8 GHOSTLY ILLUMINATION

"When we speak of light, we are generally thinking of the glaring light of glass and electricity. In the past fifty years light has progressed quite surprisingly. It is all happening so quickly that one can hardly keep up. But if we have light in greater quantity it would not have to be harsh…."

—Paul Scheerbart, *Glass Architecture*, 1914

I am interested in another kind of ghostly light, which at times occurs in the glass overlays of Smith-Miller + Hawkinson's Corning Glass Center...the conjuring up of apparitions...objects and subjects. Nathaniel Hawthorne also captured solid apparitions through shades and shadows in his architectural book, *The Marble Faun*, written in 1860.

9 The Smith-Miller + Hawkinson Corning Glass Center is a very important piece of architecture. Unique to Smith-Miller + Hawkinson's work are a number of concepts; one of them is how they juxtapose heavy steel beams (sometimes girders) in relation to the cacophony of overlayering glass, along with the powerful detailing of smaller steel sections holding the glass (angles, etc.), when all put together creating a cosmic world of floating, transparent glass at times becoming translucent (through multiple overlapping pointal metal connectors acting as stars in an evolving metal and glass world). It is like Varèse's great musical composition *Ionization*. The Smith-Miller + Hawkinson work is a densification process of glass toward reflected opacity.

10 The three individual monumental planes of solid glass supported by vertical (beautifully designed) metal pylons and supporting details is a special achievement. Jean Prouvé would certainly have celebrated these glass walls. This is radically new, a proper and exciting entry into our new century, a further extension of cubism into architecture.

11 There are two kinds of cubism, one being the solid state of opaque cubism of Braque, Picasso, and Gris, the other the transparent liquefied kind of Feininger. I have never been satisfied with the lightweight latter (although Braque captures solidified liquid in some of his late paintings). In some of the photos of Judith Turner of the Corning Center, glass transparencies become densified—in other words lightweightness moves toward a solid state. This makes a big difference. It is also necessary to feel the weight of glass, its heavy soul weight. Smith-Miller + Hawkinson have produced a new vision concerning this matter.

12 In the last scenes of Orson Welles's masterpiece, *The Lady From Shanghai*, a scene takes place in a house of mirrors. The human characters play out their lives in the multireflectivity of mirrors. A cubist triumph. The final shattering of the mirrors into shards of falling glass slivers portends the disappearance of a world.

13 While we await in anticipation the rising of the Phoenix, we remember Jefferson's poplars along a bucolic canal where one still had time to reflect in slow motion, during a beautiful late afternoon approaching evening.

—John Hejduk, Architect
New York City
October 1999

P.S. In the end, glass, mirrors, polished metals, transparencies, reflectivities, translucencies, opacities, are all absorbed by the eyes of the viewing observer.

Many years ago, my wife and I had the privilege of meeting Melina Mercouri, the then Minister of Culture for Greece. When looking into her eyes, her eyes shone with crystal intensity. They went back into deep perspective space, back thousands and thousands of years, until antiquity. She smiled, and past shadows disappeared. Her smile illuminated an essence...what it was to be miraculously human.

ARRIVAL + DEPARTURE

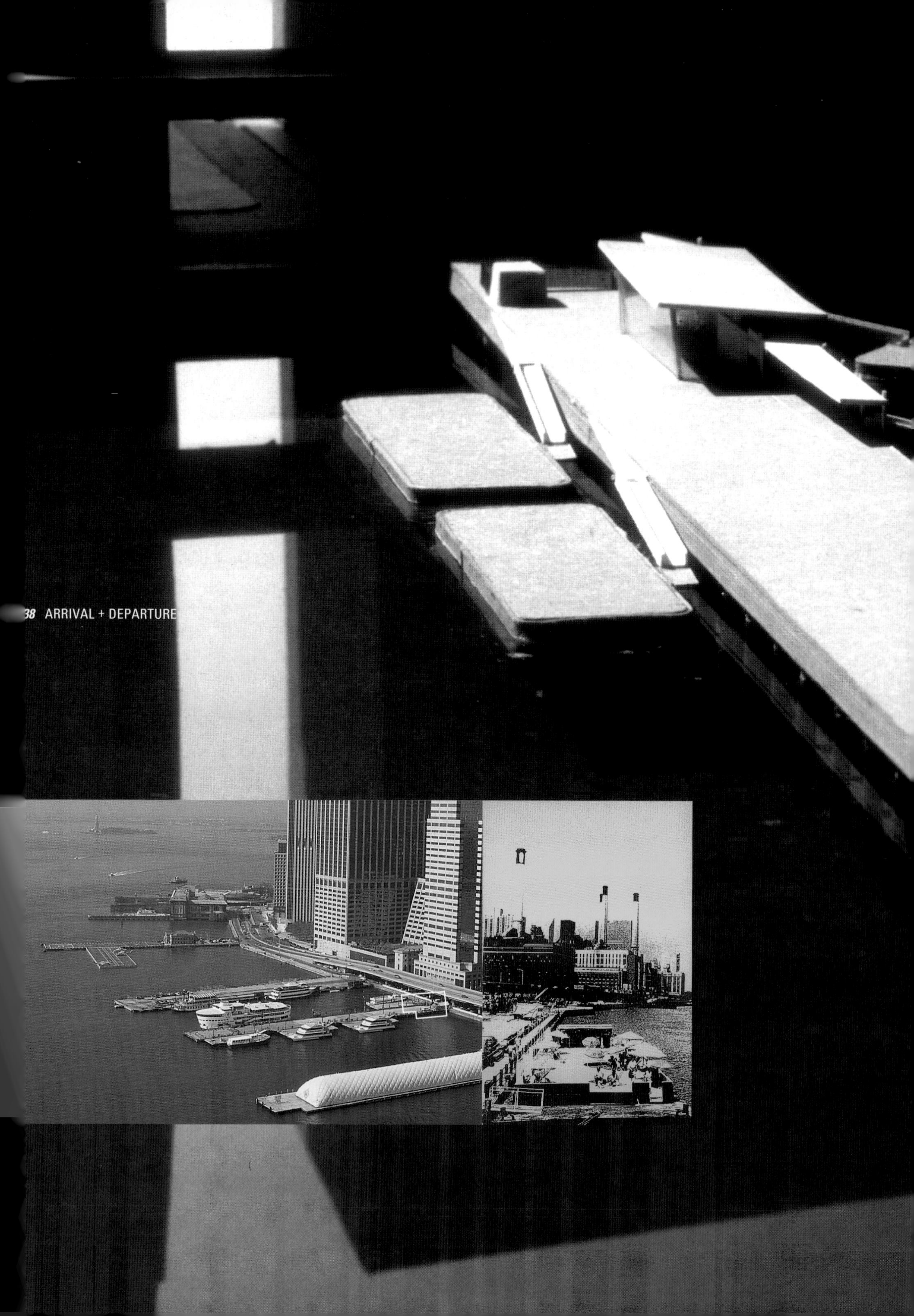

PIER 11, WALL STREET FERRY TERMINAL   NEW YORK, NEW YORK 1996–1999

ARRIVAL + DEPARTURE

This project for a building at the threshold of the city and its waterfront provides a permeable edge for East River water-based infrastructure. The structure is conceived of as a north barrier/edge to the open field of the pier surface, and is clipped to one side of the surface plane to provide a clear open space to the river. The space of the pier is kept intentionally free of objects: functional equipment intended for the terminal operations are placed along the perimeter; and highway lighting defines the space instead of filling it. A series of canopies provide a visual link from the adjacent elevated highway to the ferry landings.

The pier is a communal public space, allowing visitors welcome access to the riverfront, its views and breezes. The ferry terminal provides a Manhattan port for small-scale, private ferry services to destinations throughout the Metropolitan waterway, including LaGuardia Airport, Yankee Stadium, and Staten Island.

The building's materials include galvanized, corrugated metal, large areas of glass, and exposed structural steel, all materials functionally sympathetic to this context's construction and which are found on the working waterfront.

In fair weather the building opens to the south, erasing the line between inside and out. The sweep of the hangar door facade is articulated at the ceiling with the enclosed motor, located in the public space of the waiting area, activating this erasure as a public event.

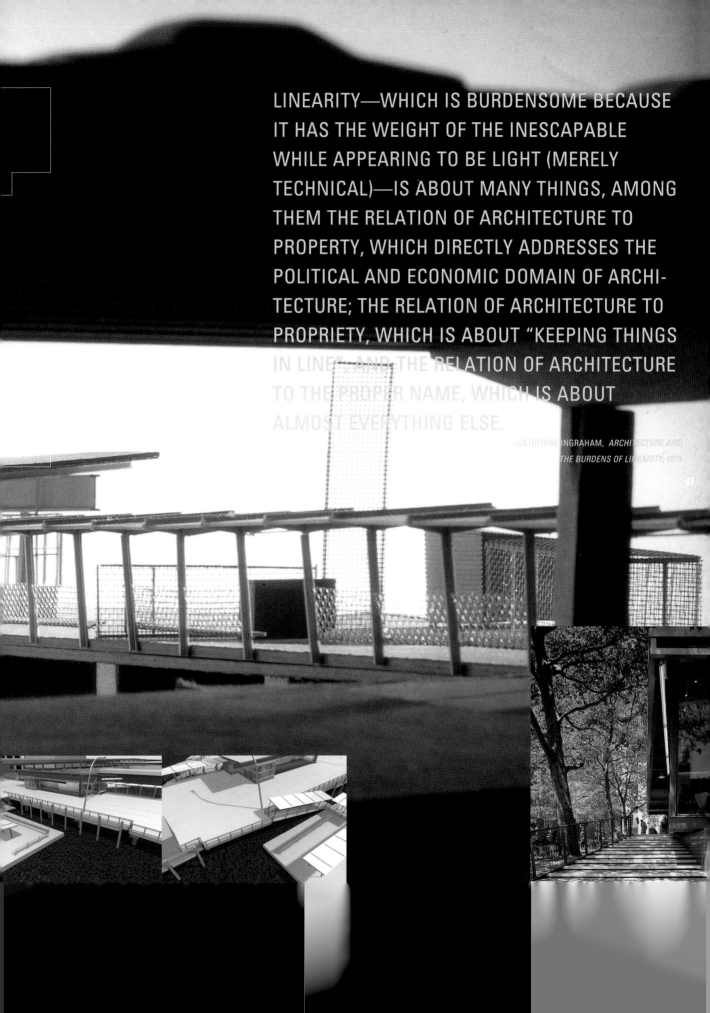

LINEARITY—WHICH IS BURDENSOME BECAUSE IT HAS THE WEIGHT OF THE INESCAPABLE WHILE APPEARING TO BE LIGHT (MERELY TECHNICAL)—IS ABOUT MANY THINGS, AMONG THEM THE RELATION OF ARCHITECTURE TO PROPERTY, WHICH DIRECTLY ADDRESSES THE POLITICAL AND ECONOMIC DOMAIN OF ARCHITECTURE; THE RELATION OF ARCHITECTURE TO PROPRIETY, WHICH IS ABOUT "KEEPING THINGS IN LINE"; AND THE RELATION OF ARCHITECTURE TO THE PROPER NAME, WHICH IS ABOUT ALMOST EVERYTHING ELSE.

—CATHERINE INGRAHAM, *ARCHITECTURE AND THE BURDENS OF LINEARITY*, 1972

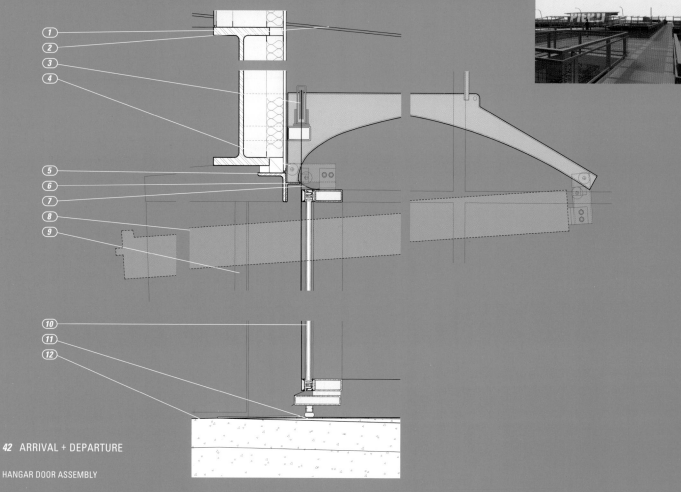

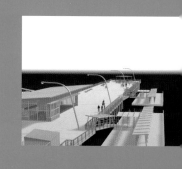

42 ARRIVAL + DEPARTURE

HANGAR DOOR ASSEMBLY

1 STEEL BEAM

2 STEEL RAFTER BEYOND

3 OVERHEAD TRACK AND PULLEY ASSEMBLY

4 TOP ROLLER

5 6"X6" STEEL ANGLE, CONTINUOUS BELOW BEAM

6 3"X4" STEEL ANGLE, CONTINUOUS BETWEEN STEEL JAMBS

7 TOP SEAL

8 LINE OF DOOR IN OPEN POSITION

9 CURTAIN WALL BEYOND

10 GLAZED HANGAR DOOR

11 STEEL PLATE AT DOOR SEAL

12 CONCRETE PIER SURFACE

13 COUNTERWEIGHT ENCLOSURE

14 HANGAR DOOR + SIDE TRACK ASSEMBLY

15 STEEL COLUMN

16 COUNTERWEIGHT ASSEMBLY

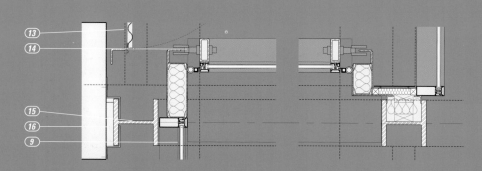

ANAMORPHIC PROJECTION

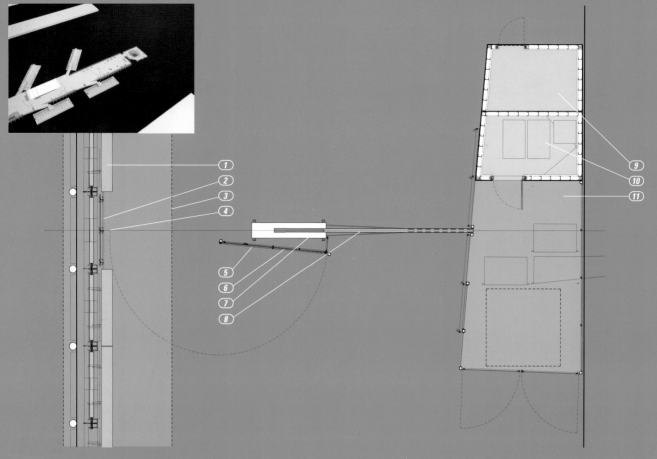

46 ARRIVAL + DEPARTURE

CROSS-PIER SECTION AT GATE

1 BENCH
2 HANDRAIL/GUARDRAIL
3 LINE OF CANOPY ABOVE
4 GATE POST

5 LINE OF GATE IN OPEN POSITION
6 CHAIN-LINK FENCE
7 TILT-UP GATE

8 HYDRAULIC TILT-UP GATE OPERATOR
9 PIER ELECTRICAL VAULT
10 PIER MAINTENANCE ROOM

11 OUTDOOR STORAGE
12 LINE OF GATE IN OPEN POSITION
13 CORRUGATED FIBERGLASS CANOPY

14 DOUBLE-ANGLE COLUMNS
15 PLATE-STEEL BENCH WITH WELDED WIRE MESH BACK
16 CONCRETE PIER SURFACE

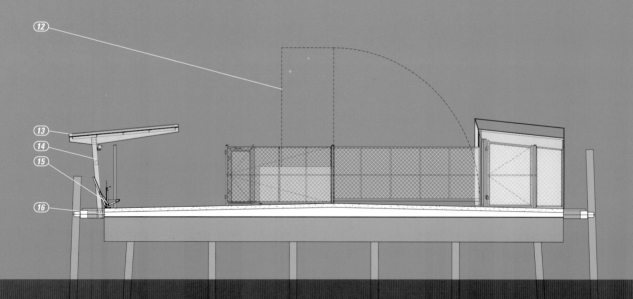

MATERIAL TRANSPARENCY

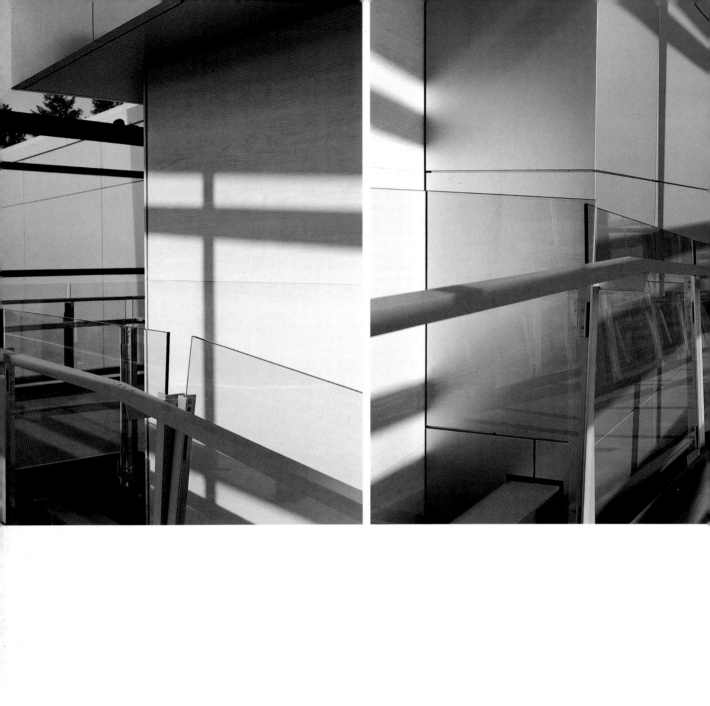

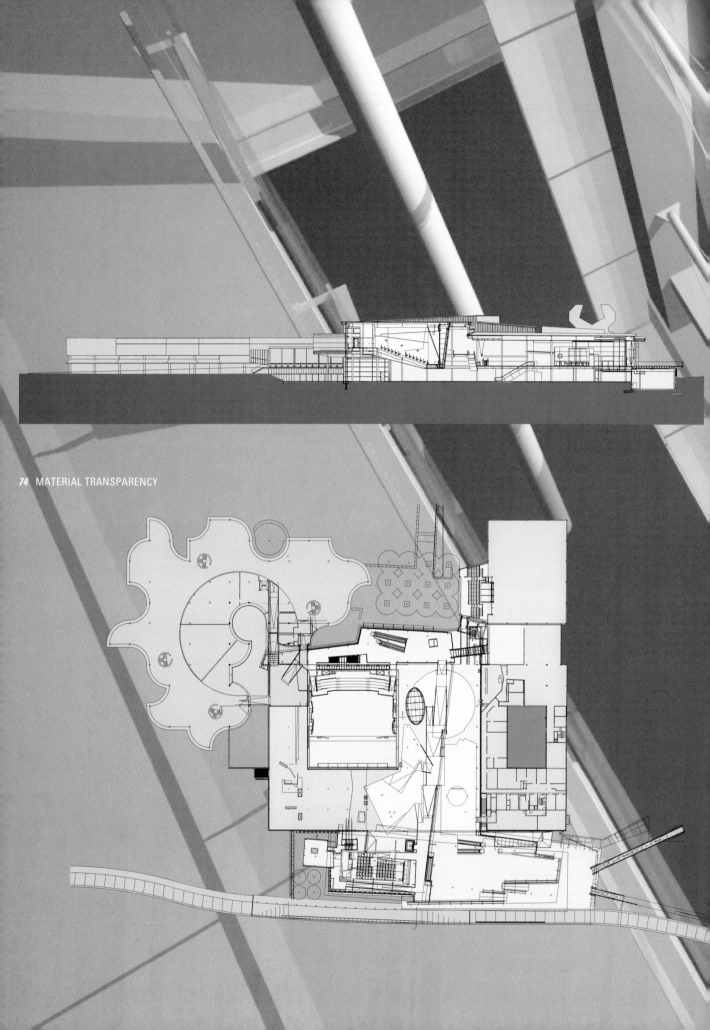

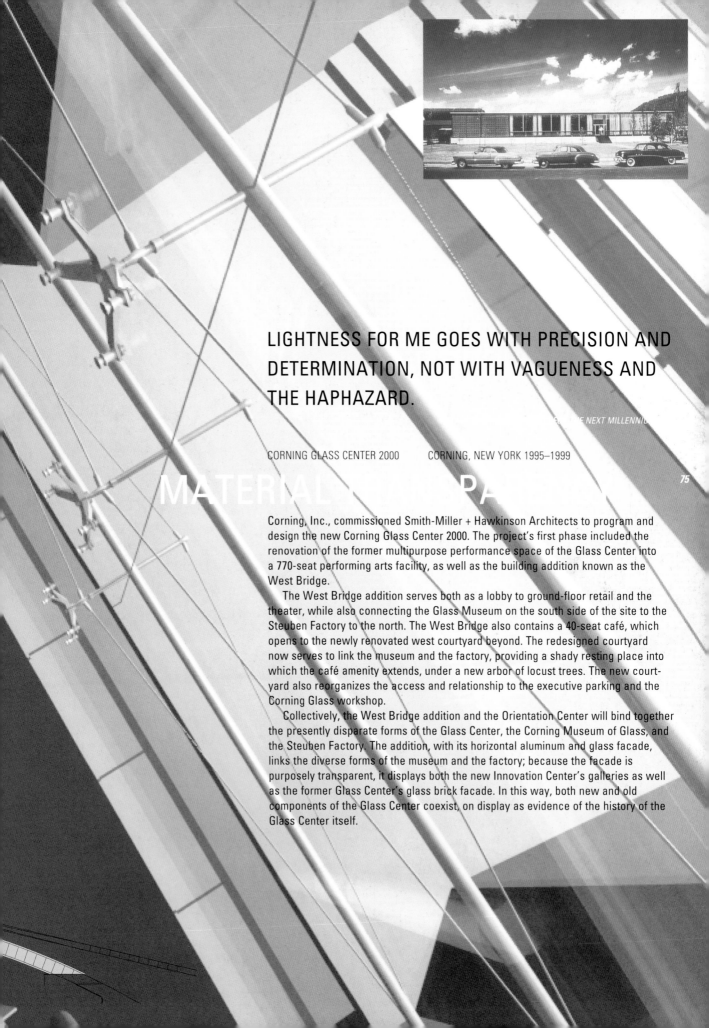

LIGHTNESS FOR ME GOES WITH PRECISION AND DETERMINATION, NOT WITH VAGUENESS AND THE HAPHAZARD.

FOR THE NEXT MILLENNIUM

CORNING GLASS CENTER 2000   CORNING, NEW YORK 1995–1999

MATERIAL   PA

Corning, Inc., commissioned Smith-Miller + Hawkinson Architects to program and design the new Corning Glass Center 2000. The project's first phase included the renovation of the former multipurpose performance space of the Glass Center into a 770-seat performing arts facility, as well as the building addition known as the West Bridge.

The West Bridge addition serves both as a lobby to ground-floor retail and the theater, while also connecting the Glass Museum on the south side of the site to the Steuben Factory to the north. The West Bridge also contains a 40-seat café, which opens to the newly renovated west courtyard beyond. The redesigned courtyard now serves to link the museum and the factory, providing a shady resting place into which the café amenity extends, under a new arbor of locust trees. The new court-yard also reorganizes the access and relationship to the executive parking and the Corning Glass workshop.

Collectively, the West Bridge addition and the Orientation Center will bind together the presently disparate forms of the Glass Center, the Corning Museum of Glass, and the Steuben Factory. The addition, with its horizontal aluminum and glass facade, links the diverse forms of the museum and the factory; because the facade is purposely transparent, it displays both the new Innovation Center's galleries as well as the former Glass Center's glass brick facade. In this way, both new and old components of the Glass Center coexist, on display as evidence of the history of the Glass Center itself.

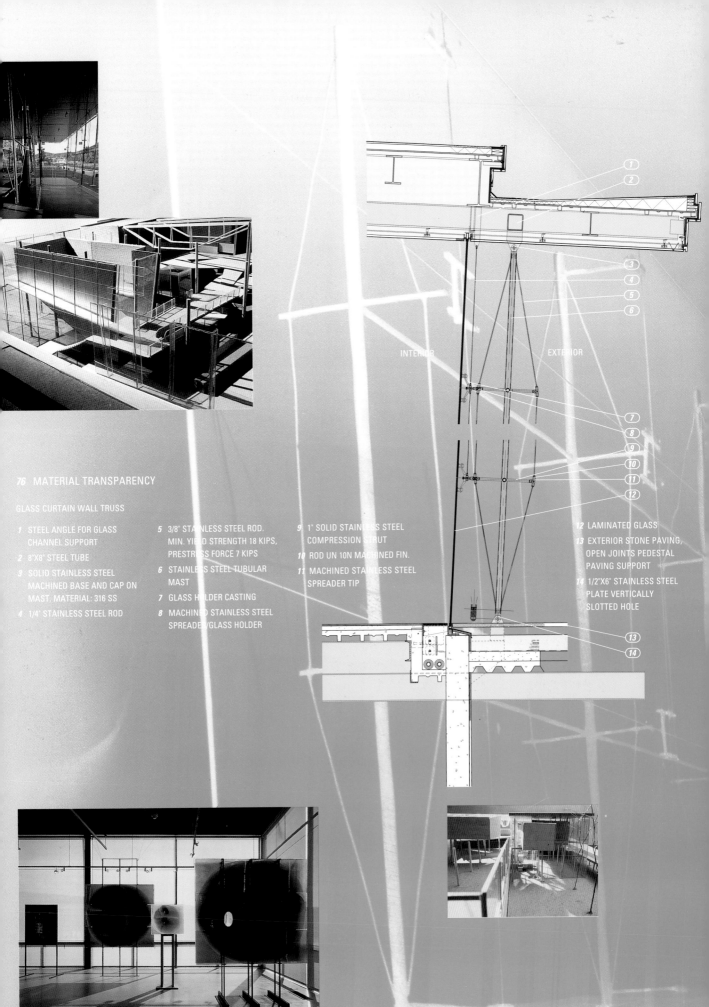

76 MATERIAL TRANSPARENCY

GLASS CURTAIN WALL TRUSS

1 STEEL ANGLE FOR GLASS CHANNEL SUPPORT

2 8"X8" STEEL TUBE

3 SOLID STAINLESS STEEL MACHINED BASE AND CAP ON MAST, MATERIAL: 316 SS

4 1/4" STAINLESS STEEL ROD

5 3/8" STAINLESS STEEL ROD. MIN. YIELD STRENGTH 18 KIPS, PRESTRESS FORCE 7 KIPS

6 STAINLESS STEEL TUBULAR MAST

7 GLASS HOLDER CASTING

8 MACHINED STAINLESS STEEL SPREADER/GLASS HOLDER

9 1" SOLID STAINLESS STEEL COMPRESSION STRUT

10 ROD UN 10N MACHINED FIN.

11 MACHINED STAINLESS STEEL SPREADER TIP

12 LAMINATED GLASS

13 EXTERIOR STONE PAVING, OPEN JOINTS PEDESTAL PAVING SUPPORT

14 1/2"X6" STAINLESS STEEL PLATE VERTICALLY SLOTTED HOLE

INTERIOR

EXTERIOR

Much like the first Glass Center at the 1939 World's Fair, the Corning Glass Center and Steuben Factory building in Corning, New York, built by the architect Wallace K. Harrison in 1951, represented a certain optimism about the future of industry and culture. These buildings represented the "best in architectural design" of their time and the Glass Center and Steuben Factory remain, to this day, landmarks of American architectural history.

The second phase of this project envisions a new Orientation Center building to the east of the present Glass Center. The Orientation Center accommodates both pedestrian and jitney-borne visitors arriving on the upper level. Seen from Centerway Boulevard, the very large glass facade of the Orientation Center offers visual access to the interior of the Center, invites the visitor to enter, and displays the Orientation (Shutterbox) Theater, the ramp at the beginning of the Glassway, and the regional exhibits.

The northeast window-wall at the main entrance of the Corning Glass Center is made of very large frameless glass plates. All glass connections, plates-to-glass doors, and plates-to-glass canopies are made by point fittings drilled through the glass. The juxtaposition of these glass window-wall components reveals the prismatic and transparent qualities of glass.

To maintain maximum transparency, the plates are supported by masts comprised of high-strength stainless-steel tension and compression members. By placing the mast interior and exterior to the glass plane, and linking the system to the building structure, the window-wall shifts from one understood as an endoskeleton to one understood as an exoskeleton—and vice versa.

The purposeful, deliberate, and didactic display of structure and glass plate at the building's entrance celebrates the visitor's passage from exterior to interior, and serves to reveal the exploratory nature of the Glass Center itself.

GLASS CURTAIN WALL TRUSS / PLAN

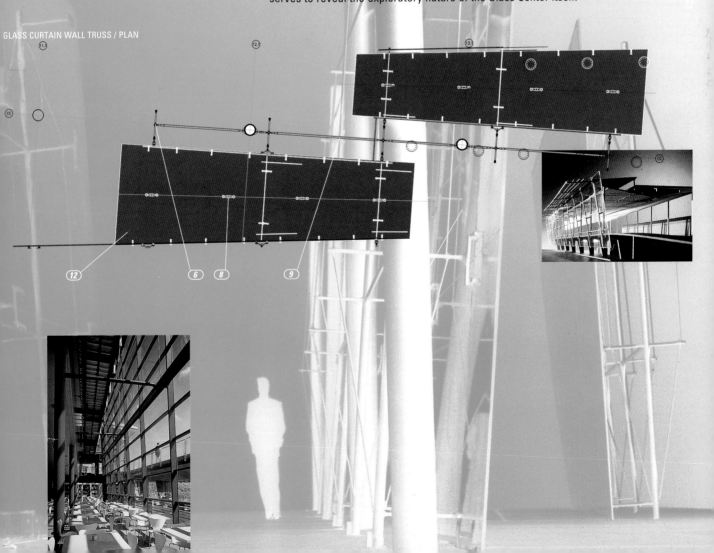

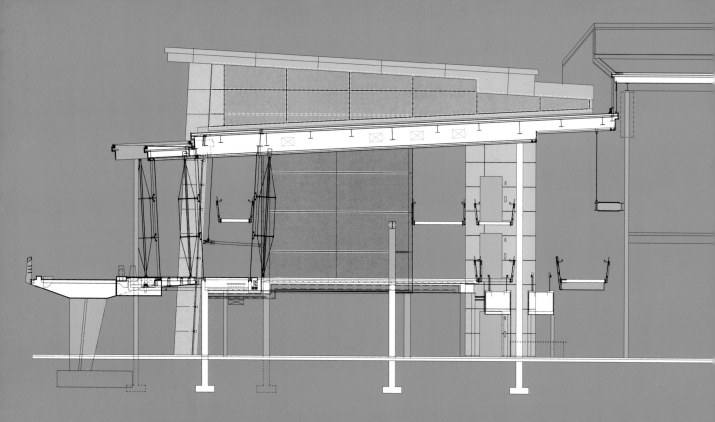

78 MATERIAL TRANSPARENCY

RAMP SECTION AT ORIENTATION THEATER

1 1/2" TEMPERED GLASS

2 1-1/2"X2"X1/4" THICK ANODIZED ALUMINUM BENT PLATE

3 3/8" THINK CUT ANODIZED ALUMINUM HANDRAIL BRACKET

4 2"X3"X3/8" ANODIZED ALUMINUM POSTS

5 1-1/2"X1-1/2"X1/4"X4" LONG ANODIZED ALUMINUM ANGLE CLIPS

6 1"X1"X1"X1/8" ANODIZED ALUMINUM CLIP

7 3/8" PAINTED STEEL PLATE

8 STEEL ANGLE SUPPORT FOR DECKING

9 MC12 STRINGER

10 STEEL STIFFENER PLATE, TYP. AT EACH HANDRAIL SUPPORT

11 1-1/2"Ø PAINTED STEEL HANGER ROD AND SUPPORT, SECURED TO STEEL PLATE

12 BUILT-UP ANODIZED ALUMINUM "T," BOLT TO STAINLESS STEEL STUDS

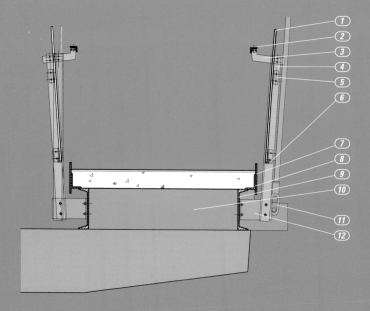

THEATER MEZZANINE AT GLASS CURTAIN WALL / PLAN

1 HANDRAIL
2 CURTAIN WALL *B*
3 3/8" THICK PLATE STIFFENER TO SUPPORT RAIL

4 NOTCHED 3/8" THICK PLATE TO SUPPORT GLASS, BOLTED TO EDGE PLATE
5 STEEL BEAM BELOW
6 CONCRETE SLAB EDGE

7 ALUMINUM GRATING EDGE
8 3/8" STEEL EDGE PLATE
9 1-1/2"X1-1/2"X1/4" ANGLE CLIP ATTACHED TO GLASS TO SUPPORT RAIL

10 3/8" STEEL EDGE PLATE BELOW
11 STIFFENER PLATE
12 CURTAIN WALL *A*

13 GLASS CURTAIN WALL TRUSS ASSEMBLY
14 TOP EDGE OF CURTAIN WALL *A*

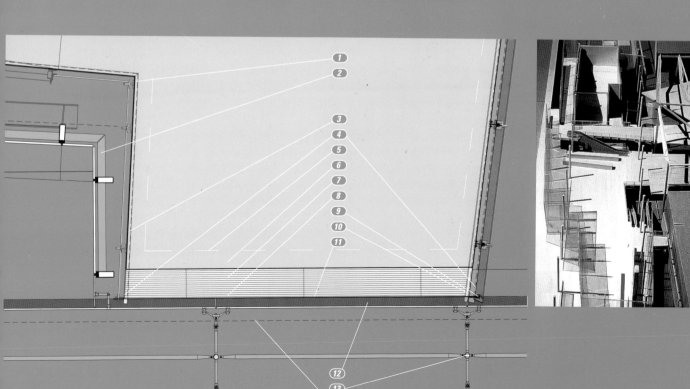

OUTSIDE IN

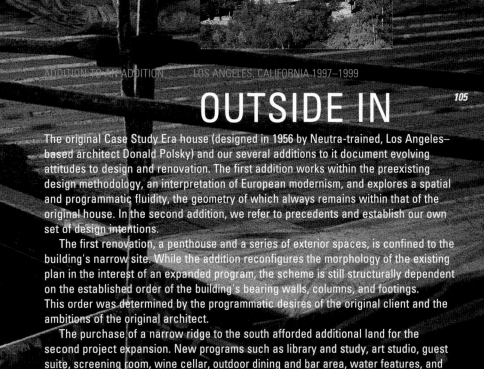

OUTSIDE IN

The original Case Study Era house (designed in 1956 by Neutra-trained, Los Angeles–based architect Donald Polsky) and our several additions to it document evolving attitudes to design and renovation. The first addition works within the preexisting design methodology, an interpretation of European modernism, and explores a spatial and programmatic fluidity, the geometry of which always remains within that of the original house. In the second addition, we refer to precedents and establish our own set of design intentions.

The first renovation, a penthouse and a series of exterior spaces, is confined to the building's narrow site. While the addition reconfigures the morphology of the existing plan in the interest of an expanded program, the scheme is still structurally dependent on the established order of the building's bearing walls, columns, and footings. This order was determined by the programmatic desires of the original client and the ambitions of the original architect.

The purchase of a narrow ridge to the south afforded additional land for the second project expansion. New programs such as library and study, art studio, guest suite, screening room, wine cellar, outdoor dining and bar area, water features, and bocce court are distributed along the top of the ridge on a shared private road.

The new buildings and their adjacent open spaces appear casually linked but, in fact, are precisely located in terms of plan and section by the positioning of topography, view, and exposure. The strategy of overlapping interior and exterior spaces both formally and programmatically was worked and reworked to enable the blurring of those borders.

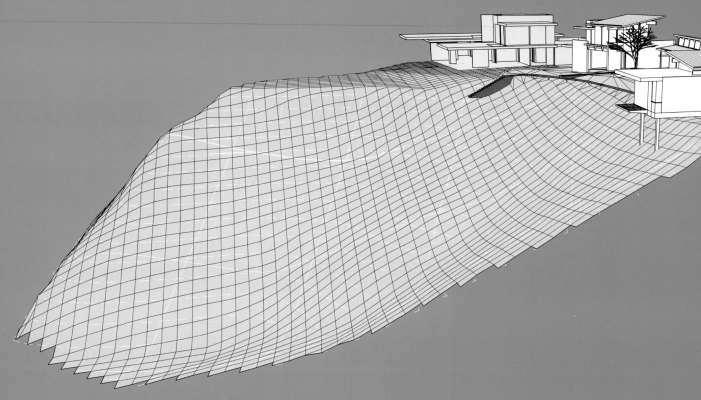

SCREENING ROOM FIREPLACE

1 STEEL PLATE HOOD
2 STEEL PLATE HOOD SHELF
3 3/4"Ø STEEL ROD DOOR PULL
4 STONE NOSING WITH
   3/8" STEEL REVEAL

5 STEEL PLATE
6 FIREWOOD SHELF
7 WINDOW
8 EDGE OF STEP IN STONE
9 STONE LEDGE

10 LINE OF HOOD SHELF ABOVE
11 3/8" GLASS AT THREE SIDES
12 10" I.D. CHIMNEY FLUE ABOVE
13 REFRACTORY CEMENT FIRE BED
   BELOW

14 MANUALLY OPERATED 1/2"Ø
   GAS VALVE
15 ADJACENT CABINETRY DOOR
16 3/8" HARDWOOD REVEAL
17 1/4" STEEL PLATE HEARTH ON
   NONSHRINK GROUT BED

18 3/4" KIRKSTONE ON SETTING
   BED AND 1/4" STEEL PLATE
19 1/4" STEEL PLATE INFILL
20 CONCRETE AT SOUTH WALL,
   WEST WALL, AND SHELF
21 1/4" STEEL PLATE SUBSTRATE

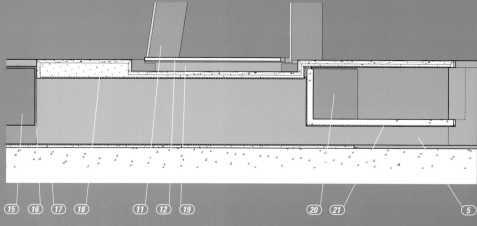

108 OUTSIDE IN

TERRACE FOUNTAIN

1 SCREENING ROOM	**4** WATER SHELF	**7** NORTH COURT	**9** PEBBLE RUNNEL	**11** KIRKSTONE BENCH
2 TERRACE	**5** LARGE POOL	**8** SMALL POOL	**10** BEACH POOL	**12** SOURCE POOL
3 KIRKSTONE SEAT	**6** BAMBOO PLANTER			

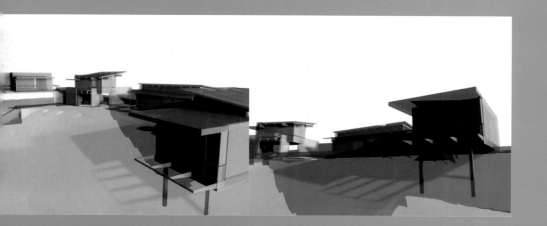

INSIDE OUT

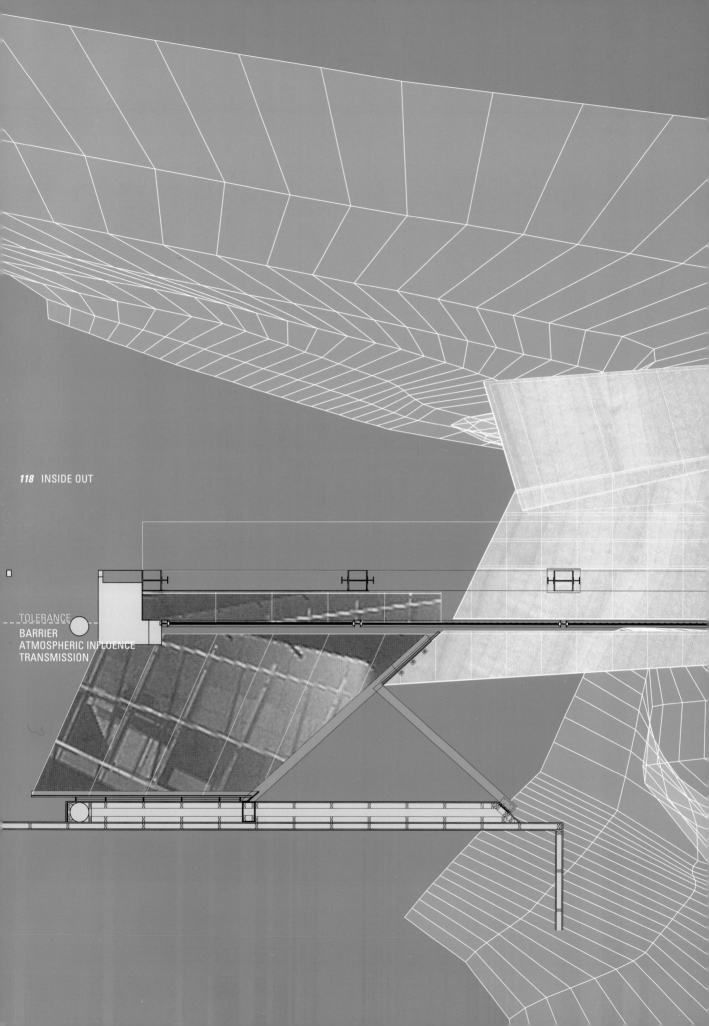

TOLERANCE
BARRIER
ATMOSPHERIC INFLUENCE
TRANSMISSION

BORDERS ARE MESSY PLACES. THEY ARE LADEN
WITH COMPLEXITY. BORDERS CONSTRUCT
PARTICULAR PLACES, THE SIDES OF WHICH ARE
NEVER SIMPLY A LINE OR LINES. —LH

FABRICATIONS　　MUSEUM OF MODERN ART　NEW YORK, NEW YORK 1998

INSIDE OUT

PERMISSIBLE DEVIATION
TRUE
RIGHT
SHELTER
DEFENSE
REVEAL

This project, part of an exhibition entitled *Fabrications*, was comprised of full-scale installations by four architects constructed in the Garden of the Museum of Modern Art, New York, January 29–April 28, 1998. The San Francisco Museum of Modern Art and the Wexner Center were also participants in the exhibition with installations at their respective locations. Aspects of each museum's installations were videotaped and included at all the locations to link the exhibitions.

A very large sheet of laminated glass and a black rubber shutter were placed adjacent to the building's exterior window-wall, in line with an exterior building column, in such as way as to reflect and display scenes otherwise purposely "hidden" from view. Inside and outside are reflected and exchanged in the eye of the observer, the shadow of the exterior shutter slides across the museum's floor and up an adjacent interior wall, while a folded plywood construct transcends the existing metal and glass facade, linking the datum of the museum to that of the garden.

The very large glass plane in the exhibit operates as a column, supporting its overhead brace, and serving as a prism to introduce oblique and hidden views of the garden. These hidden views conceal the "real" building column at the exterior. Glass, with its multiplicity of physical characteristics, serves here as semiotic element to reify the transitory and fleeting experience of culture as presented in the museum.

A TRANSPARENT BORDER (GLASS)
IS OFTEN DISGUISED AS A LINE.
TRANSPARENCY BOTH ANTICIPATES
AND COMPLICATES ADJACENCY.
THE SKIN ACTS AS A BARRIER,
A WEATHER SEAL, AND AS SOME-
THING TRANSMISSIBLE. —LH

fabrication. *n.* of action. 1. The action or process of fabricating; construction, fashioning, manufacture, also a particular branch of manufacture. 2. In bad sense: The action of fabricating or "making up"; (the invention of a statement); the forging (of a document). Also an invention; a false statement; a forgery. Truth, right. Orthogonality—the laser datum (strike a datum across and through the room). Technos—rightness

tolerance. Permissible deviation.

deviation. 1. The action of deviation; turning aside from a path or track; swerving, deflection. 2. Divergence from the straight line, from the mean or standard position; variation fig.: Divergence a.) from any course, method, rule, standard, etc. b.) Moral declension, or going astray.

protection. 1. Shelter, defense, or preservation form harm, danger, evil; patronage, tutelage. 2. A thing or person that protects. 3. A writing or document that guarantees protection, exemption, immunity to the person specified in it; a safe conduct, passport, or passage. 4. Protection from wind, fire, water—*regardez*—the gaze.

SHUTTERBOX 123

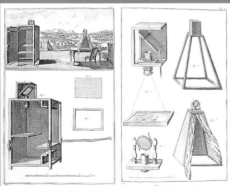

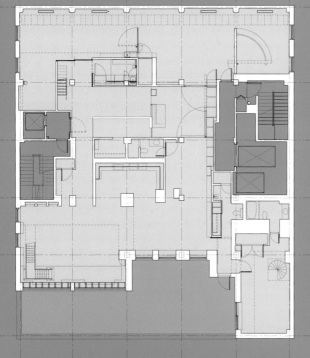

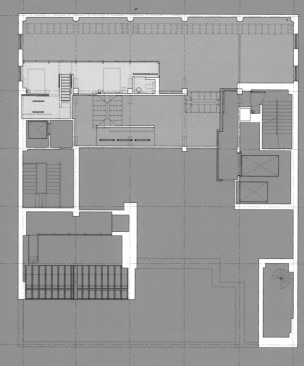

GREENBERG LOFT   NEW YORK, NEW YORK 1997

SHUTTERBOX

135

The project is a series of interventions, each dedicated to a unique set of local circumstances with particular emphasis on the attention to detail and materiality.

Located in Manhattan's Garment District at the top of an anonymous concrete building, this project houses a large private collection of "Outsider Art" as well as a residence for the owner.

Using an austere palate of glass, concrete, blackened steel, and a minimum amount of wood details, significant changes were made to the existing context. At the same time, the existing concrete shell of the loft was treated as a palimpsest for the new work.

Areas for the display of the art collection were developed to coexist with the program of living. In light of the owner's varied programs of use, we proposed "cross-programmed" spaces, the definition of which was created by lighting, very large (or moving) doors, and mechanized skylight shades.

Given the sectional constraints of the existing spaces, a new mezzanine floor of reinforced concrete was added. Spectacular views of the city were offered by a rehabilitated north-facing skylight monitor, and new glass and steel handrails were installed along with thin, structural bar hangers to support the mezzanine.

In this project the highly crafted mediating design events integrate with the existing conditions to create a third condition, one of fine negotiation and craft.

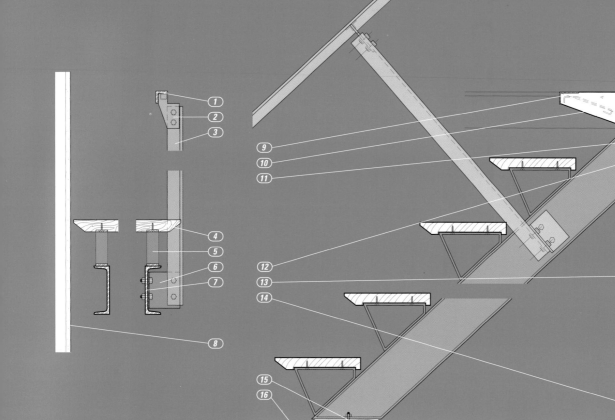

136 SHUTTERBOX

STAIRCASE TO MEZZANINE

1 1-1/2"X1-1/2"X1/4" BLACKENED STEEL ANGLE HANDRAIL. FINISH TYPICAL ALL STEEL

2 1/4" STEEL HANDRAIL WEB

3 2"X2"X3/8" STEEL POST

4 1-1/2" SOLID MAPLE TREAD

5 2"X1/4" STEEL STRAP

6 4"X3"X1/4" STEEL CLIP BOLTED TO CHANNEL

7 C8X11.5 STEEL CHANNEL

8 PLASTER WALL

9 1-1/2"X2-1/2"X1/8" STEEL EMBEDMENT PLATE

10 CONCRETE SLAB WITH TAPERED NOSING

11 4"X4"X1/4"X4" STEEL ANGLE, BOLT TO STEEL CHANNEL AND SECURE TO EMBEDMENT PLATE

12 SCHEDULED DOOR TRACK

13 1-1/2" MAPLE VENEER SLIDING DOOR LEAF

14 3/4"X3/4"X1/8" STEEL DOOR GUIDE, BOLT TO FLOOR

15 EXPANSION BOLT THROUGH REVEAL SHIM TO SLAB

16 MAPLE FLOOR OVER 3/4" PLYWOOD SUBFLOOR ON EXISTING CONCRETE SLAB

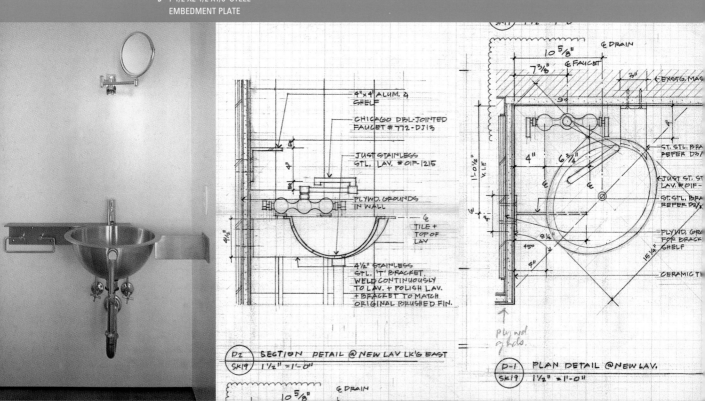

MEZZANINE HANDRAIL

1 1"X3" BLACKENED STEEL SUSPENSION COLUMN. FINISH TYPICAL ALL STEEL

2 1/2" TEMPERED GLASS

3 WT 5"X6"X2-1/4" WELDED TO CLIP

4 5"X6"X2-1/4" STEEL ANGLE WELDED TO CLIP

5 3"X3"X3/8" STEEL ANGLE HANDRAIL

6 1-3/4"X1-3/4"X1/8" STEEL CLIP

7 3/8" THICK STEEL SHIM

8 3"X4"X1/4"X4" STEEL ANGLE

9 1-3/4"X1-3/4"X1/8" STEEL CLIP

10 MC4X13.8 STEEL CHANNEL CAP ANCHORED TO SLAB

11 2"X1/4" STEEL STRAP

12 5"X1/2" STEEL ANCHOR PLATE

13 3/4" MAPLE END CAP AT PLASTER WALL

14 EXTENT OF SLIDING DOOR PATH

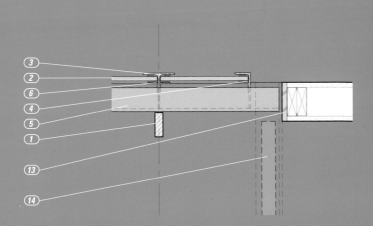

TEXTUALIZED LANDSCAPE

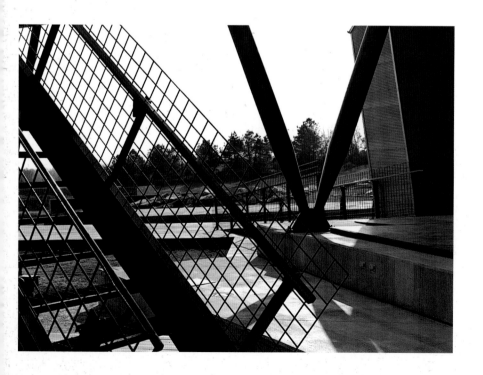

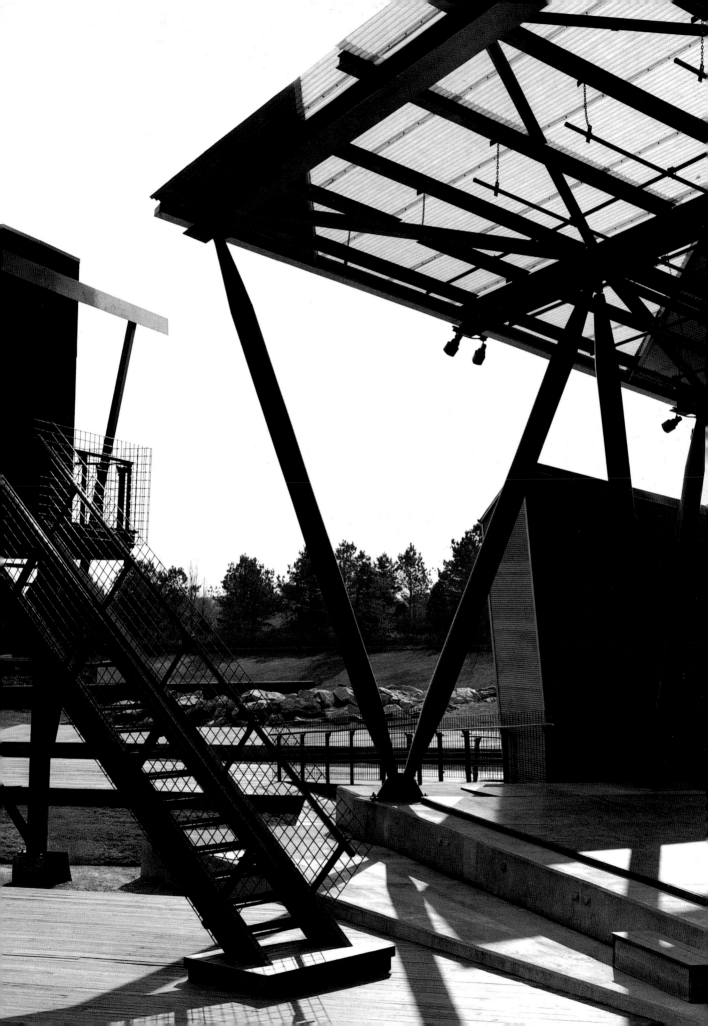

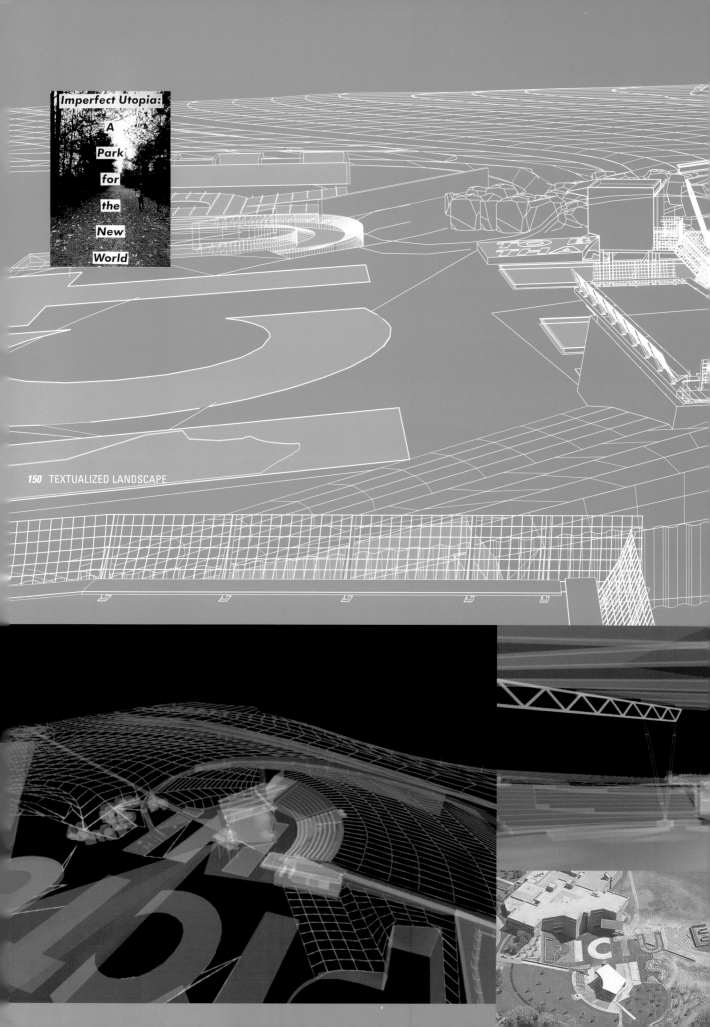

Imperfect Utopia:
A Park for the New World

THE THEORY

TO DISPERSE THE UNIVOCALITY OF A
"MASTER PLAN" INTO AN AEROSOL OF
IMAGINARY CONVERSATIONS AND
INCLUSIONARY TACTICS.
TO BRING IN RATHER THAN LEAVE OUT.
TO MAKE SIGNS.
TO RENATURALIZE.
TO QUESTION THE PRIORITIES OF STYLE
AND TASTE.
TO ANTICIPATE CHANGE AND INVITE
ALTERATION.
TO CONSTRUCT A CYCLE OF REPAIR
AND DISCOVERY.
TO QUESTION THE LIMITATIONS
OF VOCATION.
TO BE BROUGHT DOWN TO EARTH.
TO MAKE THE PERMANENT TEMPORARY.
TO SEE THE FOREST FOR THE TRESS.
TO HAVE NO END IN SIGHT.

THE PROGRAM

TO RESTRUCTURE THE APPROACH TO
THE MUSEUM.
TO ALLOW FOR LABORATORY SETTINGS
FOR ARTISTS AND DESIGNERS.
TO PROVIDE A VISIBLE, INEXPENSIVE,
SHORT-TERM BOTANICAL STRATEGY
TO ALTER THE PLACE.
TO INTRODUCE MOVIE-GOING, WALKING,
WADING, EATING, READING,
BIRD-WATCHING, RELAXING, AND OTHER
FAMILIAR PLEASURES.
TO PUNCTUATE THE SITE WITH
REGIONAL, CULTURAL, AND VERNACULAR
SIGNAGE.
TO REPLACE THE FOREST THAT HAS
BEEN LOST.

NORTH CAROLINA MUSEUM OF ART   AMPHITHEATER AND OUTDOOR CINEMA   RALEIGH, NORTH CAROLINA 1996

TEXTUALIZED LANDSCAPE

In collaboration with Barbara Kruger, artist, Nicholas Quennell, landscape
architect, and Guy Nordenson, engineer.

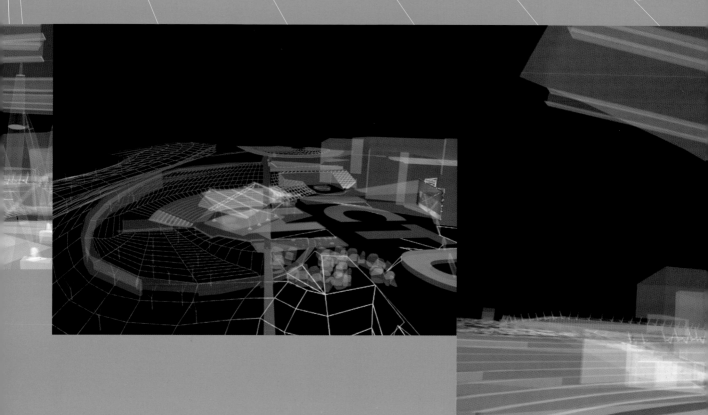

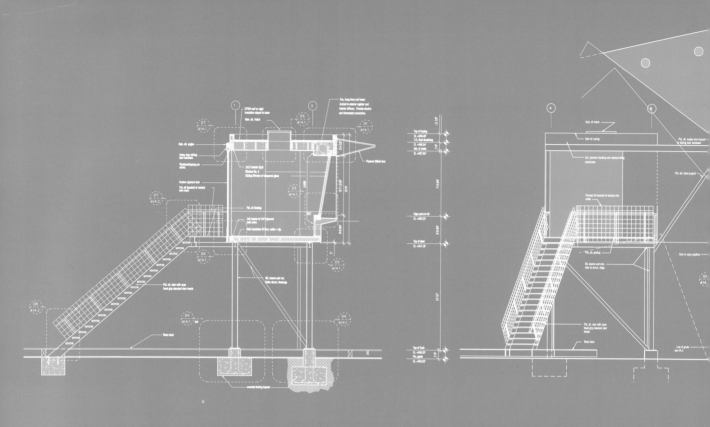

152 TEXTUALIZED LANDSCAPE

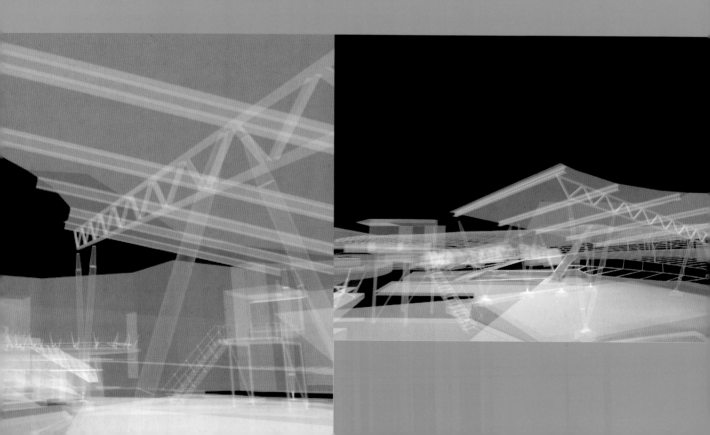

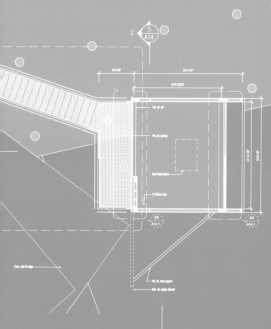

The Master Plan for the North Carolina Museum of Art involves a programmatic investigation and critique of contemporary conditions of twentieth-century art and landscape, and their relationship to a 167-acre site in Raleigh, North Carolina. The project entails the possibility of a solution beyond simple site-work, earth-moving, and the traditions of landscaping. Titled "Imperfect Utopia: A Park for the New World," equal emphasis is placed on the development of both theory and program.

The three-acre site of the Amphitheater and Outdoor Cinema, Phase 1 of the Master Plan, is located adjacent to the existing museum, and provides the first opportunity to interpret ideas of the larger plan previously developed by this team, while giving direction and structure to the phases and projects that follow.

The Textualized Landscape melds the concepts of spectacle, site, and text into a public space that expands the museum's capacity for outdoor programs. Engaging ideas of history, culture, geography, and topography, this public space provides an accessible place for a variety of experiences in the landscape. The Big Roof for the Amphitheater stage has many functions. Its sculptural form provides an identity and focus for the Amphitheater within the landscape, and accommodates an intimate outdoor gathering under one roof, protecting the performers from weather and sun. The aluminum and steel structure of the Big Screen attached to the west side of the existing museum is 30 by 60 feet, and angled for viewing from the sloped landscape in the foreground. The Outdoor Cinema accommodates 1,200 with adjacent overflow areas for an additional 1,200.

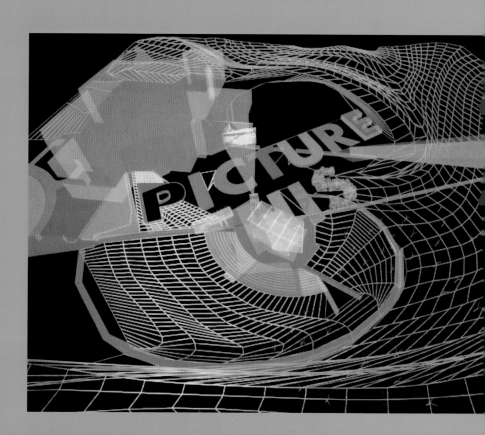

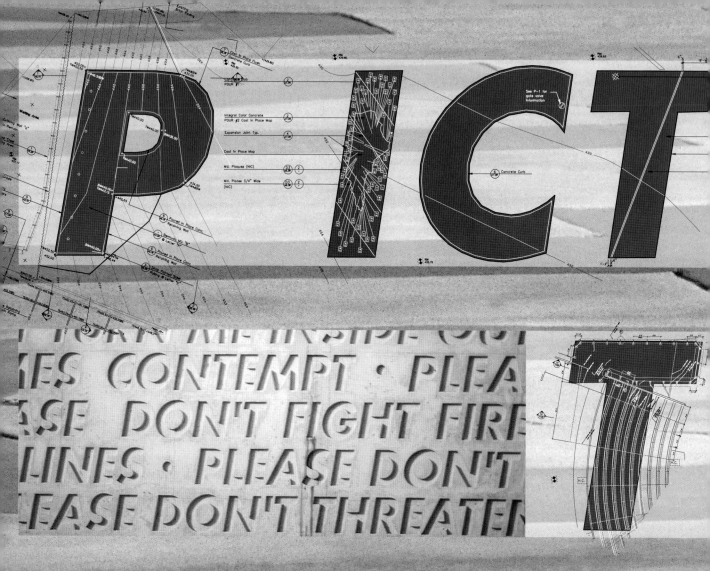

P AN EXCAVATION CUT INTO THE LANDSCAPE.
RETAINING WALL CAST WITH TEXT.
WALL IS WASHED WITH LIGHTING FROM BELOW.

I SLOPED FOR SEATING TO THE BIG SCREEN.
CONCRETE IMPRINTED WITH A MAP OF NORTH
CAROLINA AND HISTORICAL POINTS
OF INTEREST.

U AN EXCAVATION.
LANDSCAPED WITH GRASSES AND
AROMATIC VEGETATION.
GROUND LIGHTING IN THE VEGETATION.

R PARALLEL ROWS OF LOW CHAIN-LINK FENCE WITH
NATIVE CLIMBING PLANTS.

T AN OVERLOOK. EXTENDS AS A COLORED SURFACE
INTO AMPHITHEATER SEATING.
A CONCESSION/RECEPTION AREA. LAVATORIES,
STORAGE, AND LIGHTING CONTROLS BELOW.

H WOOD DECK INTERSECTS WITH THE BIG STAGE.
THE LETTER H IS COMPLETED ABOVE IN THE SKYLIGHT
OF THE BIG ROOF, CONSTRUCTED OF TRANSLUCENT
FIBERGLASS AND CORRUGATED ALUMINUM.

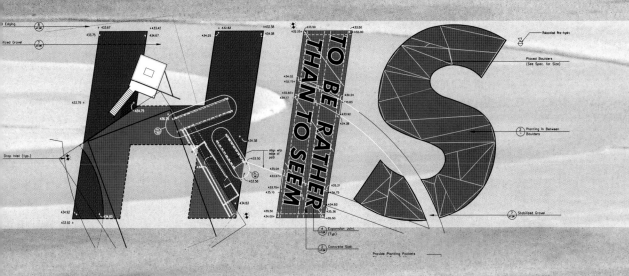

C SANDY SEATING AREA FOR THE BIG SCREEN. DETAILED CONCRETE EDGE PAINTED RED.

T A CONCESSION/RECEPTION AREA. FINISHED ASPHALT. PAINTED LINES AND REFLECTORS.

E PROVOCATIVE QUOTATIONS FROM THE IMPORTANT HISTORICAL FIGURES INCORPORATED INTO THE EXTERIOR AND INTERIOR OF AN OPEN-ENDED CONCRETE BLOCK WALL, HIGHLIGHTED BY PERIMETER LIGHTING.

I SLOPED FOR SEATING TO THE BIG SCREEN. CONCRETE IMPRINTED WITH THE NORTH CAROLINA STATE MOTTO, "TO BE RATHER THAN TO SEEM."

S A CONSTRUCTED LETTER, BUILT OF BOULDERS WITH PLANTING.

SECOND SKIN

SECOND S

The building site, located in the new central business distri
position with regard to the future of Seoul. This eight-story
three components: an automotive showroom for a new aut
world-class restaurants for an exclusive clientele, and a c
the Samsung Corporation.

The project proposes a structure of two skins: one glass, on the interior; and a second, for privacy, made of titanium plates, at the exterior.

The building is conceived as both opening up and closing down simultaneously. At the ground level, the street as a surface is extended horizontally into the building. This new surface is opened to reveal multiple spaces above and below. On the upper floors the building's exterior surface opens opportunistically, revealing specific views for interior spaces and closes to block views into the interior. This formal strategy is employed both programmatically and site-specifically. The resulting building is introspective and closed down on the upper and basement floors (the restaurants), and open at the street level (the showroom and lower-level restaurant). There are several gardens: one at street level leading from the north to the lower restaurant level, an enclosed three-story space at the southwest corner of the building at the restaurant levels, and an outdoor roof space. Smaller interior pocket gardens are developed in the space between the two skins.

At the most public part of the building, both layers of the building's skin are opened at the northeast corner of the site to expose a new automobile displayed on a raised and tilted platform, an extension of the automobile showroom level. At its most private, the building's skin, fashioned of reinforced titanium plates, offers discretion and privacy for diners from the exterior. These same plates provide the backdrop for the interior as concealed lighting washes and reveals the inside faces of the plates on the upper floors.

The building's formal strategy of opening and closing, folding and unfolding, revealing and concealing, attempts to achieve the seemingly irreconcilable conditions of continuity and discontinuity with the specifics of the site and the city itself.

PROGRAMMED AREAS

1 MECHANICAL

2 CONFERENCE

3 RESTAURANT 02 L2

4 RESTAURANT 02 L1

5 RESTAURANT 01

6 OFFICE

7 SHOWROOM L2

8 SHOWROOM L1

9 PEDESTRIAN ENTRY

10 AUTOMOBILE ENTRY + PARKING

11 RESTAURANT 03

12 PARKING RAMP

13 PARKING B3

14 PARKING B4

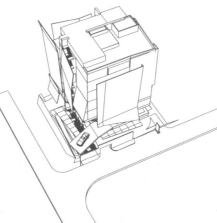

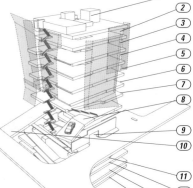

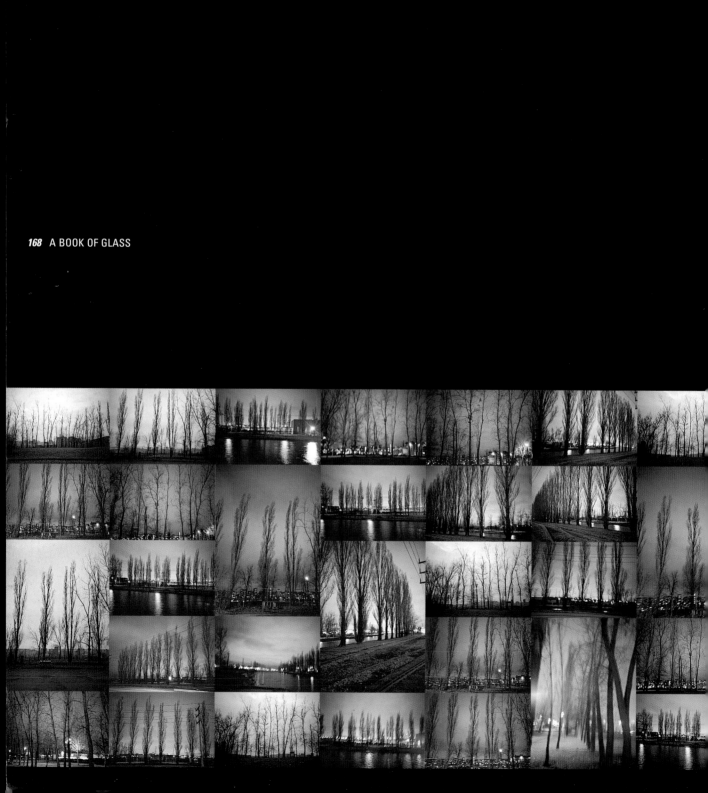

A BOOK OF GLASS

ON THE TABLE, A BOOK OF GLASS.
IN THE BOOK ONLY A FEW PAGES WITH NO WORDS
BUT SCRATCHED IN A DIAMOND-POINT PENCIL TO PIECES IN DIAGONAL
SPIRALS, LIGHT TRIANGLES; AND A FRENCH CURVE FRACTURES LINES TO
    ELISIONS.

THE LAST PAGES ARE SIMPLEST. THEY CAN BE READ BACKWARDS AND
    THOROUGHLY.
EACH PAGE BENDS A BIT LIKE LUDICROUS PLASTIC.
HE WHO WROTE IT WAS VERY AMBITIOUS, FED UP, AND FINISHED.
HE HAD BEEN TEACHING THE INSIDES AND OUTSIDES OF THINGS

TO CHILDREN, TEACHING THE ART OF REMBRANDT TO THEM.
HIS TWO WIVES WERE BEAUTIFUL AND DEATH BEGINS
AS A BEGGAR BESIDE THEM. WHAT IS AN ABSTRACT *PERSONA*?
A PAINTER VISITS BUT HE PREFERS TO LOOK AT PERFUME IN VIALS.

AND I SEE A BOOK IN GLASS—THE WORDS GO OFF
IN WILD LOOPS WITHOUT WORDS. I SHOULD
WAKE AND RENDER THEM! IN BED, MOTHER SAYS EACH CHILD
WILL RECEIVE THE BOOK OF ETCHINGS, BUT THE BOOK WILL BE
    INCOMPLETE, AFTER ALL.

BUT I WILL MAKE THE BOOK OF GLASS.

TO LAURIE AND HENRY,

DAVID SHAPIRO

ALL PHOTOGRAPHS BY
JUDITH TURNER EXCEPT
WHERE NOTED.
JUDITH'S PHOTOGRAPHS WERE
PRINTED BY DAVID WONG,
DAVID WONG CUSTOM
PHOTO LAB, NEW YORK.

ALL DRAWINGS PREPARED
FOR PUBLICATION BY
DIETER JANSSEN.

PROJECT CREDITS

ARRIVAL + DEPARTURE
PIER 11
WALL STREET FERRY TERMINAL
NEW YORK, NEW YORK
1996–1999

PARTNER-IN-CHARGE:
LAURIE HAWKINSON

PROJECT ARCHITECT:
ALEXIS KRAFT

DESIGN TEAM:
CHRISTIAN LYNCH
NAM-HO PARK
STARLING KEENE
ELLEN MARTIN
TODD ROUHE
KARIN TAYLOR
ANNE HINDLEY

MATERIAL TRANSPARENCY
CORNING GLASS CENTER 2000
CORNING, NEW YORK
1995–1999

PARTNERS-IN-CHARGE:
HENRY SMITH-MILLER +
LAURIE HAWKINSON

PROJECT ARCHITECT:
INGALILL WAHLROOS

DESIGN TEAM:
JOHN CONATY
FERDA KOLATAN
FLAVIO STIGLIANO
OLIVER LANG

PROJECT TEAM:
TOM BAKER
JENNIFER BENNINGFIELD
CATHERINE BIRD
KEVIN CANNON
ERIC COBB
PAUL DAVIS
ANNE HINDLEY
ROBERT HOLTON
MARIA IBANEZ DE SENDADIANO
JÖRN TRÜMPER
MAY KOOREMAN
ALEXIS KRAFT
CHRISTIAN LYNCH
ELLEN MARTIN
VIRGINIA NAVID
AKIRA OKAJI
MAURICIO SALAZAR
EUN SUNG CHANG
ERIC VAN DER SLUYS
IRINA VERONA
KRISTINA YU

OUTSIDE IN
ADDITION TO AN ADDITION
LOS ANGELES, CALIFORNIA
1997–1999

PARTNER-IN-CHARGE:
HENRY SMITH-MILLER

PROJECT ARCHITECT:
STARLING KEENE

DESIGN TEAM:
ALEXIS KRAFT
MARGI GLAGOVIC NOTHARD
CHRISTIAN LYNCH
FERDA KOLATAN
WANDA DYE
KARIN TAYLOR
OLIVER LANG

INSIDE OUT
FABRICATIONS
MUSEUM OF MODERN ART
NEW YORK, NEW YORK
JANUARY 29–APRIL 28, 1998

PARTNER-IN-CHARGE:
LAURIE HAWKINSON

PROJECT ARCHITECT:
FERDA KOLATAN

PROJECT MANAGER:
KARIN TAYLOR

DESIGN TEAM:
WANDA DYE
MARIA IBANEZ DE SENDADIANO

SHUTTERBOX
GREENBERG LOFT
NEW YORK, NEW YORK
1997

PARTNER-IN-CHARGE:
LAURIE HAWKINSON

PROJECT ARCHITECT:
BENNETT DUNKLEY

DESIGN TEAM:
VIRGINIA NAVID
ERIC VAN DER SLUYS
MARIA IBANEZ DE SENDADIANO

TEXTUALIZED LANDSCAPE
NORTH CAROLINA
MUSEUM OF ART
AMPHITHEATER AND
OUTDOOR CINEMA
RALEIGH, NORTH CAROLINA
1996

PARTNERS-IN-CHARGE:
HENRY SMITH-MILLER +
LAURIE HAWKINSON

PROJECT ARCHITECT:
JOHN CONATY

DESIGN TEAM:
ELIZABETH ALFORD
BENNETT DUNKLEY
ANNETTE FIERRO
MICHAEL HIRSCH
VIRGINIA NAVID
BRIAN OSTER
GREG DU PASQUIER
INGALILL WAHLROOS

SECOND SKIN
SHILLA DAECHI BUILDING
SEOUL, SOUTH KOREA
1996

PARTNERS-IN-CHARGE:
HENRY SMITH-MILLER +
LAURIE HAWKINSON

PROJECT ARCHITECTS:
FERDA KOLATAN
FLAVIO STIGLIANO

DESIGN TEAM:
CATHERINE BIRD
KEVIN CANNON
JOHN CONATY
KAWNG-SOO KIM
PHILLIP KOENEN
VIRGINIA NAVID

ALL PROJECT TEXTS WRITTEN
BY LAURIE HAWKINSON,
EXCEPT *OUTSIDE IN*
BY HENRY SMITH-MILLER.

BIOGRAPHIES

HENRY SMITH-MILLER IS AN ARCHITECT AND PRINCI-PAL IN THE OFFICE OF SMITH-MILLER + HAWKINSON.

SMITH-MILLER BEGAN HIS PRIVATE PRACTICE IN 1977 FOLLOWING A SEVEN-YEAR ASSOCIATION WITH RICHARD MEIER AND ASSOCIATES WHERE HE WAS A PROJECT ARCHITECT FOR SEVERAL NATIONALLY REC-OGNIZED ARCHITECTURAL PROJECTS: THE ATHENEUM AT NEW HARMONY, INDIANA, THE ALBANY MALL ART MUSEUM, AND THE BRONX DEVELOPMENTAL CENTER. HE RECEIVED AND UNDERGRADUATE DEGREE FROM PRINCETON UNIVERSITY, A MASTERS IN ARCHITECTURE FROM THE UNIVERSITY OF PENNSYLVANIA, AND A FULBRIGHT GRANT TO STUDY ARCHITECTURE IN ROME. HENRY SMITH-MILLER HAS HELD VISITING ADJUNCT PROFESSOR POSITIONS AT COLUMBIA UNIVERSITY, THE CITY UNIVERSITY OF NEW YORK, THE UNIVERSITY OF VIRGINIA, THE UNIVERSITY OF PENNSYLVANIA, HARVARD UNIVERSITY, AND YALE UNIVERSITY. HE HAS ALSO SERVED ON THE BOARD OF CREATIVE TIME AND IS A MEMBER OF THE ASSOCIATE COUNCIL OF THE MUSEUM OF MODERN ART IN NEW YORK.

LAURIE HAWKINSON IS AN ARCHITECT AND PRINCIPAL IN THE OFFICE OF SMITH-MILLER + HAWKINSON.

HAWKINSON RECEIVED HER MASTER OF FINE ARTS DEGREE FROM THE UNIVERSITY OF CALIFORNIA AT BERKELEY, ATTENDED THE WHITNEY INDEPENDENT STUDY PROGRAM IN NEW YORK, AND RECEIVED HER PROFESSIONAL DEGREE IN ARCHITECTURE FROM THE COOPER UNION IN 1983. CURRENTLY AN ASSOCIATE PROFESSOR OF ARCHITECTURE AT COLUMBIA UNIVERSITY, LAURIE HAWKINSON HAS HELD VISITING ADJUNCT PROFESSOR POSITIONS AT SCI-ARC, HARVARD UNIVERSITY, YALE UNIVERSITY, PARSONS SCHOOL OF DESIGN, AND THE UNIVERSITY OF MIAMI. HAWKINSON IS A BOARD MEMBER OF THE ARCHITECTURAL LEAGUE OF NEW YORK, A MEMBER OF THE BOARD OF GOVERNORS OF THE NEW YORK FOUNDATION FOR THE ARTS, AND HAS SERVED AS A PANELIST FOR THE NEW YORK STATE COUNCIL ON THE ARTS IN ARCHITECTURE, PLANNING AND DESIGN FROM 1986 TO 1989.

JUDITH TURNER IS A PHOTOGRAPHER CURRENTLY RESIDING IN NEW YORK CITY.

TURNER BEGAN TAKING PHOTOGRAPHS IN 1972 AND HAS HAD SOLO EXHIBITIONS IN THE UNITED STATES, EUROPE, ISRAEL, AND JAPAN. SHE HAS BEEN AWARDED SEVERAL GRANTS AND FELLOWSHIPS AND IN 1994 RECEIVED AN AMERICAN INSTITUTE OF ARCHITECTS HONOR AWARD. TURNER HAS HAD SEVERAL BOOKS OF HER WORK PUBLISHED, INCLUDING *JUDITH TURNER PHOTOGRAPHS FIVE ARCHITECTS, WHITE CITY, ANNOTATIONS ON AMBIGUITY, PARABLES & PIECES,* AND *AFTER.* HER PHOTOGRAPHS ARE INCLUDED IN THE PERMANENT COLLECTIONS OF VARIOUS INSTITUTIONS INCLUDING THE INTER-NATIONAL CENTER OF PHOTOGRAPHY, WHITNEY MUSEUM OF AMERICAN ART, BROOKLYN MUSEUM OF ART, THE GEORGE EASTMAN HOUSE COLLECTION, THE GETTY CENTER, THE CANADIAN CENTRE FOR ARCHITECTURE, BIBLIOTHÈQUE NATIONALE DE FRANCE, MUSEUM LUDWIG (KÖLN), TEL AVIV MUSEUM, AND TOKYO METROPOLITAN MUSEUM OF PHOTOGRAPHY.

SPECIAL THANKS TO EVE MICHEL AND ALAN OLMSTED, JAMES HOUGHTON, THOMAS BEUCHNER AND KEN JOBE, SAM FRANK, ROBERT AND EVA SHAYE, TERRANCE RILEY, ROBERT GREENBERG AND CORVOVA LEE, LAWRENCE WHEELER, AND YOUNG BUM LEE AND BRIAN K. YOUN. —LH+HSM

LAURIE HAWKINSON
HENRY SMITH-MILLER
JUDITH TURNER

EUN SUNG CHANG
JOHN CONATY
DANA CUPKOVA
LUBEN DIMCHEFF
WANDA DYE

ARCADIO GONZALES
DIETER JANSSEN
MIKE JOHNSTON
STARLING KEENE
ALEXIS KRAFT

MAY KOOREMAN
FERDA KOLATAN
ALEXANDER MORITZ
NAM HO PARK

AMANDA REESER
DAVID SOWARDS
FLAVIO STIGLIANO
INGALILL WAHLROOS